# A Line in the Sand

## A Journey Towards Forgiveness

Holly Coop

Copyright © 2021 Holly Coop
All rights reserved.

ISBN: 979-8-9911032-3-7

Cover Photo by Holly Coop
Cover Design by Mauverneen Blevins

Dedicated to those who struggle to forgive,

and those who long for forgiveness.

## Contents

Forty Years..................................................1
Waves Against the Stone..........................2
My Horizon.................................................3
Mourning Sun.............................................5
Wrecking Ball.............................................6
Deflated......................................................7
Mistakes.....................................................8
Prayer........................................................9
Adrift.........................................................10
Same.........................................................12
Truce.........................................................15
Bleak Forecasts Ahead............................16
Nothing.....................................................18
After Losing You.......................................20
Lonely Hearts Club Train.........................22
The Mercy Train.......................................24
Her ME......................................................26
Pray the Lord............................................27
What are You Reading These Days........28
Gratitude...................................................29
Five Minutes More....................................30
Karmic Footprint.......................................32
Ignite Your Life.........................................33
Neglect Your Reflect................................34
Stumbling Blocks.....................................35
Do You See What I See?.........................36
The Remedy.............................................37
Limits.........................................................38

## Contents

Clean Sweep.................................................39
Blank Space................................................40
Bedside Epiphanies.....................................41
Hope...........................................................42
Forgiving Self.............................................44
Quicksand..................................................48
Mercy This Way.........................................49
   Forgiveness...........................................51
Time Well Spent.........................................52
Pruning......................................................54
Respect Is..................................................55
Live in the Moment....................................56
That Old Familiar Place.............................57
Acceptance................................................58
If Your Brother Were to be Dead Tomorrow.....60
Is it Not Enough That I Love You?..............62
Get to the Bottom Line...............................63
Head Space – Heart Place.........................64
Here I am Lord – Ready to Heal................66
We Walk....................................................71
Tunnel Vision.............................................72
You Win.....................................................73
You Ask.....................................................75
It Takes Time.............................................76
Because I Love You...................................78
Be the Bulldozer – Not the Ground............80

Acknowledgments

To those whom, I have wronged –
*My heartfelt apologies*

To those who have wronged me –
*My wholehearted forgiveness*

To my husband, children, family, and friends who continue to love and support me, faults and all, you have my gratitude and endless love.

Special thanks to Denise, whose help untangling my thoughts to ensure more clarity for the reader was a Godsend. You continue to inspire and awe me with your gift of living life to the fullest and your ability to accomplish more in one day than most can hope to in months. You wear many hats, my dear friend, and always with a genuine smile.

Blessed is the merciful, for they shall obtain mercy.
*The Gospel of Matthew 5:5*

## Forty Years

For forty years, my brokenness caused you suffering.

You paid the price in atonement for my sins.

If I could change your life for the better,

I would give up my own so that you may live yours again.

But time does not move backward.

Past sins need not be forgiven twice.

We are promised sin forgiven,

is forever removed from His sight.

I pray for this truth for you, my dear.

Sweet child, I love you so much.

For you to forgive me once and for all,

Will free my soul to soar like a dove.

But some things are too much to wish for,

Some things are too much to ask.

Grounded for eternity with broken wings,

Alone, I sit on the shore, until the day I breathe my last.

## Waves Against the Stone

*a line in the sand has been drawn*

Can you drown in the shower under your falling tears?

Can a downpour of sorrow bring death nearer?

While I stand alone and naked, my prayer is that I will die.

Perhaps my being gone will *free them* of my life.

Besides,

is there any hope to live?

When the ones you love refuse to forgive?

Bad memories keep you enslaved.

Let the waves wash over your shame.

If lying down your life is the way theirs would be - saved

For once, be honorable, be brave.

Alone and naked in the sand,

Lie the stoned, in her grave.

## My Horizon

There is nothing to see on my horizon but emptiness.

The remnants of my hopes, my dreams,

are lost in the swirling grains of sand.

I am invisible in this world of loneliness.

Heartache is my only friend.

Looking across the horizon, I see only death.

Blackness hovers overhead.

But hope peeks out through the thickest cloud,

ushering towards me a Light.

Though blinded by the sting of tears,

In my darkness, there is a flicker of bright.

Can there be a tomorrow?

Can a new day bring death to life?

Suddenly on the horizon,

appears an angel in flight.

Soaring through the gray,

Her wings cover the sky.

Bathed in a sea of blue roses,

surrounded by souls reborn.

She brings to earth the promise of hope,

the gift of faith, the strength to cope,

with love to conquer hate.

Finally, from the dome of my destruction,

across the empty horizon,

I see the way to escape,

is to bask in His glorious light,

on the other side of the gate.

## Mourning Sun

Goodbye sunshine.

Tomorrow brings a new mourn.

Only sorrow fills my past.

Flooding my NOW in a sea of downcast.

Too many tears to cry.

Too many eyes to dry.

When a mother has let down her young.

Too many wrongs to overcome

The future is not kind to the soul,

who foolishly made choices while numb.

To such a despicable one,

the darkness of a moonless night

will be her mourning sun.

### Wrecking Ball

Maybe I was part of the demolition crew,

who left rubble in your past.

But you are driving the wrecking ball,

crushing me in its path.

You are throwing the grenade,

singeing me in the blast.

You are pouring the gasoline,

and you are striking the match.

Maybe I *was* part of the demolition crew who left rubble in your past.

But you are wasting your NOW, limiting your future by erecting walls to keep me chained behind.

By holding on to your past, you are wrecking both of our lives.

## Deflated

With every kick to the stomach, my spirit deflates a little more.

A spirit deflated cannot soar.

I am not the person in your dream.

I am the person I was born to be.

Including *all* my flaws, *fortunately*.

To say nothing is my best defense.

Stubborn pride builds strong walls.

No matter how long or far I crawl,

I struggle to escape from my past.

Maybe when I am underground,

*you* will rise above,

and set me free.

## Mistakes

The fool allows the mistakes made by others,

to rob them of their own lives.

To forgive, forget, and move on is the path taken by the wise.

Take responsibility for only your *own mistakes,*

letting those of others go.

Untie the bonds to my un-forgiven soul.

**Prayer**

Prayer is always the answer,

No matter the dilemma.

When life is at its best,

when life is at its worst.

Prayer is always the answer,

to every blessing,

to every curse.

Prayer is the answer.

For those that hunger,

for those that thirst.

Unceasing prayer can change a stony heart.

Give the lost and defeated a new start.

Prayer is always the answer,

throughout the heavens, across the earth.

In every language, *prayers* heard.

## Adrift

Depression is like being deserted on an island.

Surrounded by the mainland, you see all the *living*,

Going about their business.

Their comings, their goings, visible.

Yet they move in slow motion,

while *you* stand among them.

In a desperate effort to reach out,

you cannot touch them.

They are too far away in their state of being.

No matter how loudly you cry out for help,

they do not hear.

No matter your attempts to draw their attention,

they fail to see.

So, you remain stranded and alone.

Day after day,

Week after week,

Year after year,

you keep going about *your* business,

watching them go about theirs.

Your comings and goings are limited,

to *your* movements.

Living is not part of your dream.

You remain surrounded by a suffocating fog, adrift.

Scared and all alone,

on an island in the sea,

in a state of *depression*,

you fear is your destiny.

**Same**

Things should get better,

or maybe not.

What if the labels, good or bad

were dropped?

What if everything became - the same?

Nothing exceptional.

Just - mundane.

Long, lingering hours,

day after day,

no change.

No ups.

No downs.

Just nothingness,

stretching across towns.

Some folk work.

Some folks don't.

Because they can't.

Or because they won't.

No need for money.

Sharing earns enough.

Material wealth steals *value* from life.

Shoulder the burden of another yoke.

Everyone reaps from those that sow.

There is nothing that separates,

good from cruel.

Things should get better,

or maybe not.

Where does that leave us?

Where does that leave love?

Where does that leave hate?

Does it leave us without hope?

Does it take away our faith?

Will it rob us of being graced?

If everything and everyone was just a series of nothingness, of *same*,

could it level out the playing field of our life game?

Would it rid us of the habit of laying blame?

And would there still be those who say,

things will get better.

But maybe they won't.

Maybe there will be no good or bad.

Maybe there will just be,

same.

**Truce**

I know we are alike.

We both have a controlling nature.

We both want to be,

RIGHT.

But in the end, we are both so wrong.

Let us drop our shields and concede this fight,

Before it is too late.

When one of us is gone,

Neither will be RIGHT.

## Bleak Forecasts Ahead

Rain on my parade?

Oh, will I ever escape from their anger, their blame?

Will I be tormented to my death?

Playing the role of scapegoat,

Caged, enslaved, kept.

When will I receive a pardon?

And who are the powers that be?

Who clenches the chains of un-forgiveness?

Who cursed me into captivity?

The torrential rain of sorrow consumes.

Wading in the flood of emotions

from un-bendable, un-mendable hearts,

I am doomed.

Sorrow washes over my heart,

As lives drift further apart.

Only an umbrella of forgiveness can protect,

From the hailstorm of past mistakes,

and a deluge of regret.

Their tears soak me.

And from their sadness, my emotions fret.

Rain on my parade?

I fear sunny days are not in my forecast yet

if their choice remains, to not forget.

## Nothing

The past has passed.

There is nothing,

I can say.

Nothing,

I can do

To change it

Or its effects

On me,

Or you.

There is nothing,

Left, but forgiveness.

Nothing,

That either can do.

The future awaits our choices,

The years we have left are few.

The present is here for the living,

Which will you give your time?

In the past, REGRET rules.

In the future, it is WORRY that enslaves.

The present can be a never-ending gift,

Every second - a moment brand new,

Provided you do not return,

for either of the previous two.

For me, the voice of wisdom speaks clearly.

I am giving up *then and there* for HERE

I can no longer live in *your* past *or* mine.

And the future requires far too much energy and time.

The only way for ME to function and thrive

is to live in the NOW where I am fully ALIVE.

## After Losing You

Wearing black because I feel blue

Lost and lonely after losing you.

Time will tell if I have strength enough,

to get me through the days ahead,

for they will be long and rough.

Missing, crying, regretting, dying,

are just some of the words I will use,

to describe my feelings after losing you.

Life does not always prepare us,

for when IT chooses to leave.

But God promises we can bear it

when we lean on Him and believe.

The days are long.

The nights belong

to my pillow.

It wears my tears.

The deluge I held back all day

while I kept myself in gear.

Now, the moon allows me to weep.

So, in my pillow, I bury the grief.

Until the morning sun wakes,

with her promise of a new day.

Refreshing my mood with the warmth of her embracing rays.

I know somewhere in the heavens, for *this*, and for me

you pray.

After losing you,

I will go on because you want me to.

On the outside, I will carry on,

my grief only visible to *me*.

On the inside, I will be wearing black,

Because of the way I feel.

After losing you,

I lost a part of me too.

## Lonely Hearts Club Train

There is a crisp in the air.

The sky is bursting with clouds.

Hazy with puffs of silver, blue, and gray.

Their presence serves to remind,

On the approaching winter days,

When time stands still,

Hearts become frozen in limbo,

just like icicles hanging off the panes of windows.

The grayness of those drawn-out days,

Only add to a body's gloom,

Reminding of lurking doom.

It is a time for the broken-hearted to ease through

their suffering in *shame*.

With guilt in tow, they ride alone

on the Lonely-Hearts Club train.

Will the salve of time protect wounds?

With scars constantly pricked.

By those who hold their hearts captive,

By choosing not to forgive?

What is a troubled soul to do to escape their tightening grip?

But stare blankly up at a hazy sky, with puffs of silver, blue, and gray.

Perhaps they will find the forgiveness they seek

Aboard the Lonely-Hearts Club train.

There is a crisp in the air,

Where time stands still.

And hearts remain frozen - in time.

## The Mercy Train

That's enough!

I have no more room for your baggage.

I have far too many bags of my own.

I wish to throw it all in the dump.

And hide behind the stones you have thrown.

I cannot change the past.

The future is not for me to see.

Time is not a promise.

We can only own this moment, to be.

Experience the now and breathe.

Unpack the bags that weigh you down.

And that includes your carry-on.

It is the way to a new start.

Fill those empty places in your heart,

Make space for more faith

Remember, sometimes you must walk through the cutting winds

before sunshine graces your face.

Fill your old baggage with gratitude.

Take your seat on His mercy train.

Fill your heart with forgiveness.

Accept His ticket to grace.

Forgiving and forgiveness go hand in hand.

If you do not forgive, you will not experience forgiveness.

And if you have found forgiveness in another heart,

you must forgive others too.

That is what holds us back,

When we cannot walk away from our pasts.

We leave behind emotional crumbs that lead us back down the same old path,

Where we continue carrying those worn-out bags.

For your baggage, I have no room.

But my heart will always have space

for the love that I have for you.

### Her Me

Lord, help me to be the woman I was born to be.

The one who has been waiting in captivity,

With her voice kept silent,

From her fear to speak,

the one in whom she failed to believe.

Lord, help me to find,

to realize,

the soul of that woman has always been.

Give her the courage to live.

Give her space to breathe,

Lead her through doors of opportunities,

and face her fear to succeed.

Strength to finally set her free,

Free to be,

Her -

ME

### Pray the Lord

Forgive and forget the bad stuff.

Stop pondering. Stop pouting over the past.

Do not dwell on the have-nots.

Just be grateful for the haves.

When sorrow visits, grieve.

Then swiftly let go of sadness.

Release the floodgates of joy.

Saturate your heart in gladness.

Always have excitement for the future,

While enjoying your life in the NOW,

Awaken yourself to this wisdom.

And if unable, pray-the-Lord – show you how.

## What are you Reading These Days?

I decided to turn over a new attitude,

instead of a new leaf.

Rather than turning the page to a new chapter,

in the same book,

I decided to shelve that one and open a fresh new read.

## Gratitude

With Every Matter, Give Thanks *No Matter*

When feeling,

Depleted,

Defeated,

Despondent,

if approached with a mindset of gratitude,

With ease, you will pass right through.

Just by incorporating a few short words,

Throughout an ordinary day,

Like bless you,

Thank you,

Excuse me, and please.

With an attitude aligned more with gratitude,

You will notice a shift,

A change.

### Five Minutes More

I would lie in bed watching your belly rise and fall.

Your eyes flutter back and forth,

As you dream through a snore.

Five minutes more,

I would cradle you in my arms no matter the mound of chores.

For in the next blink of my eye,

You will be exiting our front door.

Five minutes more,

I would vocalize my gratitude.

And apologies would hold less weight,

Then the words I love you will compensate.

I could not have asked for a better mom or dad,

Then who I was blessed to have had.

But through hurried visits, the moments passed,

And now just five more - oh, how I wish I had.

Five minutes more,

I would articulate my heartfelt thanks.

For the many gifts You have given,

And the sacrifice You made.

Five minutes more,

My lungs will breathe their last,

My eyes will wake to an open gate,

To the home, You have prepared.

And with Your arms stretched wide, awaiting my return,

As I reach out from my unclenched fists,

To Your eternal open hand,

My soul will rejoice - AT LAST!

I could not have waited,

Five minutes more.

## Karmic Footprint

Good karma, bad karma.

Everybody has karma – to give and *to get*.

Attitude versus Gratitude.

What fills the mood of your day?

The answer will define the karma you exhale.

When the wind blows it back in your direction,

the latter may prevail.

Attitude versus Gratitude.

Choose wisely the rules of your day.

Because karma comes back around –

the exact route from which it came.

Good Karma. Bad Karma.

Everyone gives. Everyone gets.

*Which* is up to you

### Ignite Your Life

You cannot be a beacon of light in the present,

If you let regrets of the past extinguish your spark.

Remember, every day is a fresh start.

Your future waits,

Embark.

## Neglect Your Reflect

Do not look in the mirror.

Look beyond the mirror.

To look *at* the mirror, you only see yourself.

You are blind to others

if you *can* see their reflection,

It is always *behind* your own.

Put others in front of yourself.

Watch your reflection change its form.

View the surroundings from a position other than your own.

## Stumbling Blocks

To minimize stumbling while moving forward,

Avoid looking back.

## Do You See What I See?

Shift your perspective from its usual frame of ME focus,

And surround yourself in the view.

Open your eyes to the world as others see it,

And you may notice it is not always about you.

When you explore with a wide lens,

A new picture takes shape.

A clearer vision emerges

A chance for real change.

### The Remedy

No healing comes from guilt and blame.

Only out of forgiveness can new beginnings dawn.

Growth will follow once we allow ourselves,

to forget and move on.

### Limits

Why let jealousy,

Rivalry,

All the other dramas,

Of life,

Limit you?

They only serve to obscure your view.

Why allow those walls to surround

The place where your freedom is unbound

and your joy is found?

Why let those brick walls form around you?

They block the vibrations created to flow.

Love.

Joy.

Energy shines.

The only thing that limits

is time.

## Clean Sweep

What is growing under your rug?

What dirt?

What grime?

Whose heart did you ransom – for your crime?

No need to blame.

No need to weep.

Just pick up the rug,

And sweep.

## Blank Space

If we do not make people hurt from our words,

Or feel fear with the actions we take,

If, when we see another human being reaching out

We do not allow our hands to pull away,

Perhaps a new world will begin to take shape.

Until then, we will continue to get back,

Not what we *need*,

to open our hearts to receive.

But an infectious attitude of - *take*,

Leaving our hearts filled,

with blank space.

## Bedside Epiphanies

Life is not about financial wealth,

But for whom our treasures helped.

Life is not about power possessed

By gaining labels of success.

It is about those our generosity blessed.

It is about the impact we leave on the weary

drowning from our thoughtlessness.

In a world immersed in greed

selfishly left on our streets

declining from their grief.

Life is not about you or me.

Life is about us

and the hearts we touch.

If we lead our lives with this in mind

Simply, live life being kind.

There will be no need for epiphanies at our bedside

## Hope

Frequently hope does not come in the form we want

Sometimes hope comes from a different direction

and opens doors to dreams

better than we had hoped

And we find that this life, as we know it,

offers more than we had thought.

Even when all hope is lost,

And worries transgress into despair,

Hope, when not within our reach, remains there.

Through a veil of pride and with hearts unaware,

We often cannot see the issues that require our care.

So, God, with his infinite love,

Begins the task of stripping our egos bare.

Only our hearts remain.

Though tattered,

by a thread, we hold on.

With our vulnerabilities slain open to ridicule and stares,

The only way to cope,

Is to see in the distance,

That glimmer of hope.

## Forgiving Self

I keep praying that I will find true joy.

I keep asking why I have not found it.

And I realize,

I am standing in its way.

My constant reminders to myself,

My mind-chatter pointing out my faults,

Leaves, very little room for *joy* at all.

Why do I hold myself to such standards?

And who set them?

Were they set by society or by You?

By my misguided thoughts, askew?

Is that not the reason for Your life?

Is that not the reason for Your sacrifice?

Are we not all here to *make* mistakes?

So, we might learn?

So, we might change?

I am no better, no worse.

I am merely the same.

My moral compass may be off at times.

But I am never walking above or below,

any other living soul.

I am no better, no worse.

I am simply among them.

I tormented Your heart,

In a garden where You sat alone.

In a courtyard with garments thrown

I held a strap in my hand,

That slashed an innocent, Godly man.

I weaved the crown of thorns,

They placed upon Your head, with ridicule, with scorn.

I watched tears stain Your cheeks,

With the skin of Your face torn.

I did not offer to help,

While You carried our cross,

Through crowds of insults-yelled

downcast was my gaze held.

I was there with a spike in hand,

When You spoke of the forgiveness of man.

But I did not offer my shoulder to comfort the Mother You gave.

And my cowardly eyes looked *away,*

When You cried out to Your Father in dismay.

I was no better, no worse.

I was among them,

That day.

And if,

After all of this,

I know to *self* must ask,

How can I possibly *not* forgive?

When You so graciously and bravely,

Forgive *me,* all of this?

I was there, too

I was a witness at the tomb when the rock moved.

My face felt the radiance of Your presence,

By the miracle of Your resurrection.

I was only one of many,

of all colors,

of those in want,

of those with plenty.

I was a blind man,

A woman stoned,

A girl left holding Your garment,

Healed from her blood flow.

An orphaned boy watched as You walked by,

Your reflection glistened in his tear-filled eyes.

When You offered to ALL,

Your peace,

Your love,

Your joy –

I was no better. I was no worse. But *I* was among them.

## Quicksand

I am feeling defeated, unable to move.

Sinking in a time warp.

Unable to get into my groove.

Every time I step into my stride,

I get stuck in another puddle.

Life has become such a struggle for even the strong to survive.

In a world of air, land, and sea,

An ocean of quicksand suffocates me.

How will I flee?

Do I dare try?

Or is my only escape,

To concede defeat,

Let the quicksand bury me,

Alive?

## Mercy This Way

Thank you for Your mercy, Lord –

Your *true* forgiving grace.

Help me, Lord, to forgive others *that* way.

To put the past in its place –

Turn my attention away.

For although my lips speak, I forgive

In my heart, the hurt remains.

My *mind* begs to forget,

But some memories leave scars slow to fade.

When will *true* forgiveness be deposited into my memory bank?

Where is the invisible gateway to freedom from the past?

Where will I find the open road that leads to a fresh start?

What is the *secret*, Lord, to a merciful heart?

If I could find my way, Lord,

through the darkness that haunts my every move,

If painful memories would not fog Your guiding light,

Perhaps my heart would finally know

how *true* forgiveness feels.

Thank you for *your* mercy, Lord –

Your *true* forgiving grace.

I pray someday I will forgive others *that* way.

## Forgiveness

Transform the heart that beats in me to love as the heart that once beat within you.

To be generous with my love

Put another's feelings above

tattered, broken, and hurt feelings of mine.

Continue to do this, time after time.

Give my memory the wisdom to know the hurting is who hurts.

The tongue that spills insults thirsts

When this desert journey is too much for my broken heart to bear,

Please allow my blind eyes to focus through the fog,

to see You waiting there.

Your mercy opened for all to give and to receive.

For our redemption was the reason

Your pierced heart and body *destined to bleed.*

Mankind freed.

## Time Well Spent

We get so wrapped up in our daily lives.

We forget what is important

What is *real*

What is *right*

A moment spared seems too much to ask.

Unaware *that* moment could be our last.

We hold on to grudges, *our* hurt feelings –

front and center in our thoughts.

Most times, we cannot remember

The reason we fought,

Others were hurt, too.

No one is perfect.

Not even you.

So, cherish the moment that is *here* and *now*.

Learn to forgive some way, somehow.

Tomorrow may be too late to apologize to a friend.

For some, it is a beginning, but for others, the end.

With your loved ones - take advantage of precious hours and precious days.

Speak the words you know you should say.

Kisses at the door might press your time –

But will be dearly remembered by those left behind.

## Pruning

Pick away those weeds that tangle around your heart

Make a little breathing room for love's fresh start

## Respect Is

Hard-earned.

Lost-easily.

Returns-rarely.

So

If you have it —

Do your best to keep it, and if you have already lost it —

Let it go — Start all over again.

Use what you *now* know.

Give the *character* a chance for regrowth.

Through all, remember that forgiveness, and that includes yourself — is the only key to *hope*.

## Live in the Moment

To live in the *past (so to speak)* - is not allowing forgiveness into your life.

– the forgiveness of others as well as the forgiveness of yourself.

To live in worry for the *future* is not trusting God.

Living in the *present* is a gift – open it every morning with joy.

## That Old Familiar Place

I am not going to visit that old familiar place.

I have walked down those corridors too many times,

And I know it is an unfriendly space.

I am sorry for anything I did that made you angry and sad.

I have apologized, asked your forgiveness,

And there is nothing more I can do about all of that.

The ball is now in your court.

It is up to you to *forgive*.

Or you can remain burdened,

Continue to waste life away,

Rather than be grateful for the life you're blessed to live,

And spend it enjoying every day for the gift that it is.

## Acceptance

I accept others.

See the good in others first.

Why not then for myself?

Why do I hold such high standards in my mind *for me* than I do for everyone *else?*

I know that reaching such expectations is next to impossible.

Why can I not leave behind judgment for the woman I call *me?*

Why can I not simply embrace her?

Accept who I am.

Reflect on the good I'm blessed to share with the world,

Spending every day doing the best that I can.

If that is all I expect from others,

Why not for myself?

When will I stop beating myself down every time I fall?

For others, a helpful hand is freely there to lend.

To myself, I point my fingers, refusing that rules can bend.

When will I give myself a break and accept the person *I am?*

When your self-approval relies on other eyes,

The outside frame is all that you see.

Acceptance begins on the inside,

Before the outside can reflect who is ME.

## If Your Brother Were to Be Dead Tomorrow

Would you want the memory of the last words spoken to him to be - you are an asshole?

You may justify it in your mind (your ego) that you were right in your observation.

And that the words spewed were words deserved.

But time will not heal the pain, and lying to yourself will not mute the pangs of truth your conscience will whisper.

It will speak to you in your dreams by sending you nightmares.

It will speak to you through *habits* that you form over the years.

It will remind you of those truths with every addiction that latches onto you.

There will be no escaping your fate.

Be humble when pride disguises remorse.

Life has a way of drifting off course, the bumpier our karmic path.

Learn the impact of your words,

They scar when other egos bruise.

Hurtful words you speak, you cannot take back.

Their pain will be the baggage *you* drag.

Hurt breeds more hurt.

It is a vicious cycle.

The only escape is up to you.

You can stop the cycle.

If you so, choose.

Observe from a distance,

The whole picture will come into view.

Everything that happens is a chance for us to learn.

This journey is a small step towards a much bigger, brighter life.

We have the choice to endure by turning away from strife.

Hurtful words are undeserved even if justified

By ego-convincing words.

The ultimate loss will be peace.

## Is it Not Enough That I Love You?

Or does my heart have to bleed every time we speak?

What is it from me that you seek?

And if I am unable to be all of that in which you dream,

How will this strained relationship ever be all that it could be?

Is it not enough that I love you?

And can you accept and love ME?

## Get to the Bottom Line

I am letting past regrets steal away happiness.

My present gets pushed aside.

I cannot possibly enjoy today if the past is where I choose to waste precious time.

This moment, this breath, this thought,

Now is my only time.

Enjoy the moment you are in,

that is the bottom line.

## Head Space – Heart Place

Even when the pieces of your life,

Crumbled to the ground,

You stood.

With your head on straight,

And your heart in place,

You stood.

You survived.

You gathered the broken pieces of your chipped, bruised, shattered, spattered heart.

Drawing from lessons of life,

You gained the courage needed for another fresh start,

time after crushing time.

Remembering who you are,

On another new journey, you embarked.

It is not easy to see the light when engulfed by the dark.

It is scary, but you have done it afraid.

You stood,

With your head on straight,

You kept your heart in place.

## Here I am Lord – Ready to Heal

she was a little girl

acting out in search

of attention not received

in her innocent world

she found ways to cope

when visited by the hurt

when she could not understand why

and from who she could not hide

young perception can be so blind

wrong to most

the young see right

she had no concept of time

until much later

when she would realize

everything has its time

for hurting

for learning

for knowing

for sharing

for being alone

for crying

and for joy

for healing and feeling

when for so long the only sensation

was that of numb

she was an adolescent

not knowing what was happening inside

afraid of all the onlookers

she wanted to run

to hide

he touched her while she was unaware

uncertain about her space

he took her under his care

she learned from his embrace

her identity formed in that place

her fate took on a new shape that day

her life now forever changed

always landing in another place

only to find the same man,

with a different face

although she did not know

she was running all alone

from a different body

from a strange face

pain became her embrace

none felt like that first touch

non left her feeling the awe

that old familiar feeling

for so long, it had been gone

she grew old

*life* charged all its tolls

evident by her creases and folds

today, those premature experiences

are memories of old

but first love scars can burn

often, hearts never heal

from those early wounds

the pains we hide easily show

through the elixirs we choose

residue from heartache can settle

in the bottom of a bottle

our darkness illuminated

by long days and late-night hours

sugar becomes our chosen vice

it serves to hide a body

disguise the hurt

but now the time has come

to leave the past behind

so, to the heavens, she cries

*Here I am, Lord, ready to heal. I have earned my place, laid claim to my space and I stand tall, ready to take my bow.*

it has taken her a whole lifetime

but finally, she has learned how

## We Walk

Our journey takes us down many roads,

And many challenges show their face.

But through the thickest part of the forest, we walk,

Our steps can be lighter with grace.

We will no doubt cross many bridges,

And some we will burn down, too.

But at the end of our darkened tunnel,

We will see a glimmer,

And in that instance, we will know,

We had been guided the whole way by You.

## Tunnel Vision

I had to go through the dark tunnel to get to the light.

Now that I have,

I think I will survive.

**You Win**

I feel dead inside

Though my heart, broken beats.

Your voice pierces the mind,

its deafening drums to remind,

my mistakes from earlier times.

I cannot shake off the remorse.

I try, but shame reminds me again.

My soul clings to hope,

My body and mind, from the inside out,

feels only death.

For how many rounds must I stay in the ring?

You have already beaten me badly.

Proven again, fight after fight,

I am not the heavyweight champion.

I keep trying to crawl my way out,

Allow you to crown yourself, winner.

Only to be dragged right back in.

With every bout, my frailty mounts,

And my will to survive grows thin.

You have won round after round.

How many more fights must I bear?

There is hardly anything left of me.

My frame of mind is but a ghost

of what my spirit once was.

From words flinging my ego to the ropes,

My soul left my body a long time ago.

Verbal abuse scars from emotional beatings,

Reality is painfully coped

Only left in your champion ring.

Is the weight left from your words

Long after, their venomous sting.

So, I concede, in this my final round, defeat.

## You Ask

What is the secret to freedom from the past?

LET IT GO!

But what to do

when it keeps following you

home?

## It Takes Time

Forgiveness

It is not about the person in need of forgiveness,

It is about the person in the position to forgive.

Hurt, rarely forgotten.

Chains of blame are not easy to release.

Only time holds those keys.

Like a silver teapot tarnished from years of neglect,

From its surface and crevices being unkempt,

Rubbing off the layers of grime -

It takes time

And so it is with our relationships,

Years of hurt,

Layers of mistrust,

Settle in crevices of broken hearts,

Leaving our lives bound in love to crumble apart.

Restoring tarnished hearts to shine,

It takes time.

Forgiveness

It is not about the person in need of forgiveness,

It is about the person in the position to forgive.

Hurt, rarely forgotten.

Chains of blame are not easy to release.

Only time holds those keys.

## Because I Love You

Through the brokenness of your heart,

I see your loneliness.

In the echoes of your mind,

I hear your fear.

In the quiet of your step, I feel you walk to me.

And with open arms, you're drawn near.

Within your vulnerable heart,

I sense your love for me,

and your fear that it has not always shown.

In the quiet of your heart,

I murmur to your soul -

Rest assured; I have always known.

The path I have laid for you may not be straight,

And you may stumble as you learn to navigate.

You may not know which way to go.

Because I love you, I put many forks on the road.

I will make straight either path you choose to take,

I will work everything out for the good of all

For the children, I have called

And in the quiet of My step, I will hold you as you walk.

And with open arms, I will catch you when you fall.

Because I love you

## Be the Bulldozer ~ Not the Ground

Until you stop seeing yourself as a victim

you will never get anywhere in life.

You did not have it any worse

than anybody else growing up.

Or maybe you did, but,

Everyone has fallout in their life.

From which the debris is not always easy to discard.

Emotional wounds leave painful scars

The secret to success,

is to leave all of it in the dust.

Move forward,

Plow past,

Be the person in your dream.

Reimagine your ME

Issues that paralyze,

Transform them to be what propel you.

Leap into a new today.

Stop letting the past prey upon your future.

Forgive,

Forget,

Move on.

Be the bulldozer, not the ground.

## A note from the Author

I believe life is a series of growing pains. We are given this lifetime on earth to learn and grow.

It is a journey we all must navigate. On our path of learning and growing, we often get hurt by and hurt others.

The pain we inflict on others stems from the pain we have experienced. It seems like a vicious cycle with no purpose. But because the one who created us for a purpose allows the hurt to happen, we can trust, *though at times difficult*, that there is a reason for everything, and as it is said - everything has its season.

The most authentic and unconditional love grows from painful hurt and suffering. We know this to be the truth by being a spiritual witness to what we know Christ endured for us on the cross. We all fall short, but though we do, He still loves and forgives us. If our hearts remain open to receive His undying love and we open our minds to believe what our eyes cannot see but our hearts can feel, we too can endure whatever hurt comes our way. And we can forgive those who hurt us, and ourselves for those sorrows we have caused others. Life is too short. Do not shorten yours by holding onto grudges and harboring hurt feelings. Let go, be free. Forgive, forget, and move past all that. Hold on to only love in your heart and have peace. *~ Holly Coop*

The following pages contain excerpts from some of my other publications and a little bit about myself.

From my book:

Heart Strings – Forever Wanderer

*Soul mate, passion mate, breathe with me through all eternity.*

A reflection of my heart in your beautiful soul drew me to look more deeply at the path I had been on and awakened me to my truth, where fate took my hand and led my wandering heart to you.

### Picking Up Pieces

I fear that you will break my heart

And there are not enough pieces left

To break apart

My head is screaming run away

My heart is leaping directly in the way

Of the pierce, from your love's aim

### Fire Starter

I know I am playing with fire

But the warmth keeps drawing me in

What harm is there in wishful thinking

If I do not

Sin?

The elements are against me

I cannot win

When love's flame ignites a lonely heart

To the passion that stirs within

I know I am playing with fire

But the warmth keeps drawing me in

How can a lonely heart defend

From a burning desire so intense?

My logic whispers

Stay away

While my heart screams

Jump right in

In the Palm of

I feel as though I hold a lot of hearts in my hand

And that I am deserving, of none

I pray I make the right choice of whom

I hand over my own to

Who will be the ONE?

From my book:

Locks of Love – A Book of Encouragement

Hopes Bright

Life

Stolen from us when we are feeling submerged in depression, a deadly current.

Hope

A life jacket God gives us.

When darkness grows thicker around us,

Hope is a distant brightness

just barely visible to our naked eye.

It appears to be surrounded by and covered with a veil of darkness.

It glistens but is unreachable from our grasp.

But through the delicately woven fabric of emotions, we can see its bright persistence to shine through.

As we trudge through our darkness, we frantically reach to pull away the veil, but the fog of gloom that suffocates us keeps pushing us back, further away from Hope's shining force.

A will of perseverance that is not our own pulls us through the debilitating thickness of our night.

The veil lifts just enough to fill our lungs with a resuscitative gasp as if we were drowning, our lungs now emptied of their liquid death; we are finally able to breathe in the freshness of a new day.

Faith pushes, while the brightness of Hope pulls us through the darkest patches of our journey, and Grace gives us nourishment while we trudge through Life.

## A Gentle Rain of Tears

What makes a grown woman cry?

Just about anything

at any given time.

Whenever we feel weary, broken, and alone,

To wash away the heartache.

Let tears flow

To clear out the crevices where despair gets trapped

In the darkest areas of our souls.

Like a gentle rain, our tears cleanse,

Until once again, we feel whole.

The Roads We Choose

Rough roads are never the paths we choose for ourselves. They are simply a reality of the journey of our natural lives. God allows these detours that lead us to the narrow path, where He awaits

About the Author

Holly Coop resides in the Midwest with her husband, children, and furry friends.

Holly enjoys writing and publishing inspirational poetry, motivational quotes, and spiritual insights. She has authored five poetry collections. Touching hearts with words has become her life purpose. She hopes her words will stir hearts and inspire others in their purpose. In addition to writing, Holly enjoys sketching, photography, and creating art featuring her poetry.

HollyCoopBooks.com

Thank you, I appreciate your support.

For more inspirational words and nuggets of wisdom,

I invite you to visit my blog HollyCoopAuthor.wordpress.com

Blessings

The End

*Is but the beginning*

*When we choose to forgive.*